KU-213-146

Are You TOUGH Enough?

Paul Mason

www.raintreepublishers.co.uk

Visit our website to find out more information about **Raintree** books.

To order:

☎ Phone 44 (0) 1865 888112

📄 Send a fax to 44 (0) 1865 314091

💻 Visit the Raintree bookshop at **www.raintreepublishers.co.uk** to browse
   our catalogue and order online.

First published in Great Britain by Raintree, Halley
Court, Jordan Hill, Oxford OX2 8EJ, part of Harcourt
Education.
Raintree is a registered trademark of Harcourt
Education Ltd.

© Harcourt Education Ltd 2006
The moral right of the proprietor has been asserted.

All rights reserved. No part of this publication may be
reproduced, stored in a retrieval system, or
transmitted in any form or by any means, electronic,
mechanical, photocopying, recording, or otherwise,
without either the prior written permission of the
publishers or a licence permitting restricted copying
in the United Kingdom issued by the Copyright
Licensing Agency Ltd, 90 Tottenham Court Road,
London W1T 4LP (www.cla.co.uk).

Editorial: Lucy Thunder and Richard Woodham
Design: Victoria Bevan and Bigtop
Illustrations: Darren Lingard
Picture Research: Melissa Allison and Kay Altwegg
Production: Camilla Crask

Originated by Dot Gradations Ltd
Printed and bound in China by Printer Trento srl

ISBN 1 844 21462 1
10 09 08 07 06
10 9 8 7 6 5 4 3 2 1

**British Library Cataloguing in
Publication Data**
Mason, Paul
Are You Tough Enough?: Body systems
613.7'1
A full catalogue record for this book is available from
the British Library.

Acknowledgements
The publishers would like to thank the following
for permission to reproduce photographs:
Corbis pp. 6–7, 8–9 (Reuters), 16–17 (Leif Skoogfors),
20–21 (Jim Sugar), 22–23 (Sygma), 28 (The Military
Picture Library/Alistair Wright); Department of
Defense pp. 28, 28; Getty Images pp. 24–25, 26;
Getty News p. 14–15; Military Picture Library
pp. 4–5 (Peter Russell), 12–13, 18–19; Reuters
p. 10–11 (Simon Kwong).

Cover image of a soldier on an assault course
reproduced with permission of Associated Press
(Luis Romero).

The publishers would like to thank Nancy Harris
and Harold Pratt for their assistance in the
preparation of this book.

Every effort has been made to contact copyright
holders of any material reproduced in this book.
Any omissions will be rectified in subsequent
printings if notice is given to the publishers.

The paper used to print this book comes from
sustainable resources.

Disclaimer
All the Internet addresses (URLs) given in this book
were valid at the time of going to press. However,
due to the dynamic nature of the Internet, some
addresses may have changed, or sites may have
changed or ceased to exist since publication. While
the author and publishers regret any inconvenience
this may cause readers, no responsibility for any
such changes can be accepted by either the author
or the publishers.

DUDLEY PUBLIC LIBRARIES
L -48005
682599   SCH
J613.7

Contents

Some words are printed in bold, **like this**. You can find out what they mean on page 30. You can also look in the box at the bottom of the page where they first appear.

Are you tough enough?

This man is training for one of the world's toughest jobs.

He is training to become a soldier. How do people become strong enough to fight in the armed forces? They have to train. They have to get their whole body working better! All their body **systems** must be in great shape.

The soldiers' **muscles** have to be strong so that they can move quickly and carry heavy packs. Their **hearts** have to work hard to carry blood around their bodies. They need to be able to breathe in enough air.

Soldiers must train hard ▶
before they can go into battle. The training is not easy. Many recruits drop out because they are not tough enough.

heart   muscle that pumps blood around the body
muscles   parts of the body that allow a joint to move
system   parts of the body that work together to do something

Would you be tough enough to train like this?

Support systems

Trained soldiers have to carry a lot of equipment with them.
A soldier's pack can weigh up to 45 kilograms (100 pounds).
Most of us could not carry this pack to the end of the street!
How can a soldier's body support all this weight?

Our **skeletons** make it possible for us to carry heavy weights.
The skeleton supports the body. It is a **system** made up of
a lot of strong bones. An adult's body has about
206 bones in it. They are linked together
to make a skeleton. The skeleton can
move. It can also carry weight.

The contents of a soldier's pack:
- clothes
- water
- towel
- cooking gear
- ammunition
- tools
- first-aid kit
- waterproof poncho
- gun

The skeleton

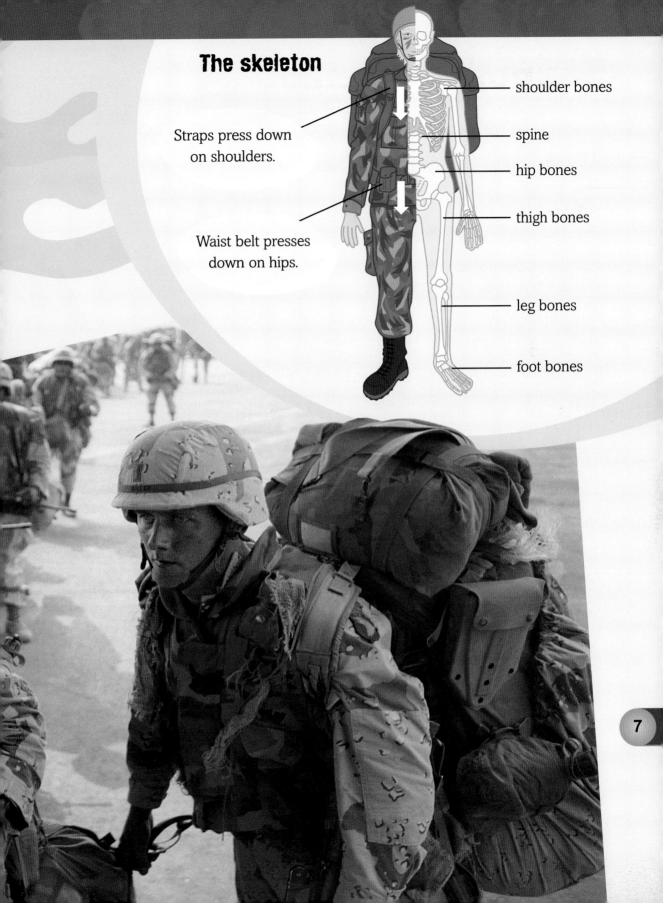

Straps press down on shoulders.

Waist belt presses down on hips.

shoulder bones

spine

hip bones

thigh bones

leg bones

foot bones

Moving along

Of course, the soldiers on page 7 are standing still. Just standing still with a pack isn't too hard! But a soldier has to move around with a heavy pack, too.

Soldiers might have to march to a new camp. They might have to crouch down to avoid being seen.

Soldiers use their **joints** to move and bend their bodies. Joints are the places where the bones in the **skeleton** are linked. The simplest type of joint is called a hinge joint. We have hinge joints in our knees. Hinge joints can only bend in one direction.

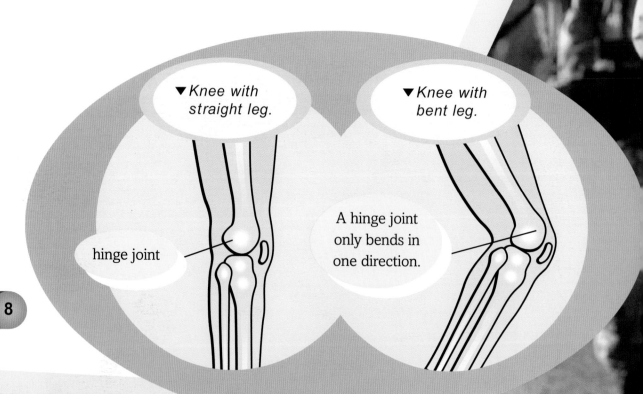

▼ *Knee with straight leg.*

▼ *Knee with bent leg.*

hinge joint

A hinge joint only bends in one direction.

joint   place where two bones are linked together

9

▲These soldiers are on patrol. They are carrying heavy packs. Each soldier's joints are being tested to the limit as they walk.

Paratroopers are ▼
some of the world's
toughest soldiers.

Making the jump

Paratroopers need to bend their knees as they land. But they also use other **joints**. When paratroopers land they have to:

- lift their arms *above* their heads to control the parachute

- reach their arms *across* their bodies to check equipment.

These movements would be impossible if shoulders had the same joints as knees. Knees can only bend in one direction. Shoulders use a ball-and-socket joint. This kind of joint can move in many different directions.

Different joints

- *Hinge joints can only bend in one direction. Knees have hinge joints.*

- *Ball-and-socket joints can move in many directions. Shoulders and hips have ball-and-socket joints.*

Muscle power

Paratroopers have to jump from heights of more than 4,600 metres (15,000 feet). When they land they must be ready for action. Only the toughest are chosen to join!

A safe landing:

1. Bend at knees and waist.
2. Tuck chin into chest.
3. Keep elbows at sides.
4. Allow thighs and waist to absorb shock of landing.
5. Roll forwards.

contract become smaller and tighter

Parachutists use their leg **muscles** to make the landing feel softer. They land with slightly bent legs. The landing makes the knee **joint** bend more. The parachutist's thigh muscles resist the force. They take in some of the shock from the fall.

Muscles can only **contract**. This is why we need at least two muscles for every moving joint. One muscle pulls the joint bent. The other muscle pulls the joint straight.

Leg muscles

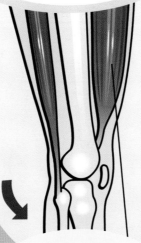

▼ This shows what happens when you straighten your knee.

Your knee straightens when this muscle contracts.

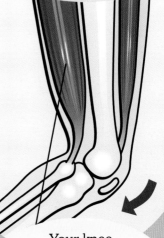

▼ This shows what happens when you bend your knee.

Your knee bends when this muscle contracts.

Gym test

Muscles control more than just your knees. A **system** of muscles controls all your movements. Muscles move your eyes. Muscles move your tongue. Muscles move your fingers and your hands. Muscles in your **heart** pump blood around your body. Muscles make your body work.

Soldiers must make sure that their muscles are strong. They have contests to test how strong their muscles are. One of these is the pull-up contest. The soldiers do as many pull-ups as they can in two minutes. The soldier who does the most pull-ups is the winner. Try it yourself and see how you do!

relaxed biceps

What happens in a pull-up?

1. The biceps muscles contract to bend the elbow joint. The body is pulled up.

2. The biceps muscles start to relax as the elbow joint straightens. The body is lowered downwards.

3. The muscles get ready for the next pull-up.

contracted biceps

Out on exercises

These soldiers are practising "advancing". Advancing means moving forwards. This is an important skill for soldiers. One day they may have to advance through woods, streets, or forest. They have to learn to do this safely.

These soldiers are ▶ learning how to advance, or move forwards, as safely as possible.

16

energy ability to move something or to do work

Exercise like this is very tiring. This is because exercise uses up the body's **energy**. The body gets energy from food. The soldiers are tired and hungry at the end of training. They need to eat to get more energy.

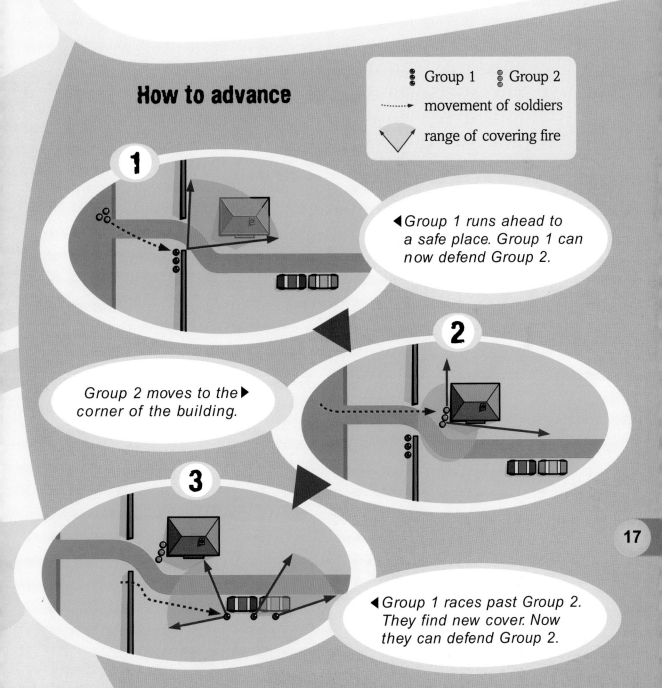

How to advance

Group 1   Group 2
········▶ movement of soldiers
           range of covering fire

1

◀Group 1 runs ahead to a safe place. Group 1 can now defend Group 2.

2

Group 2 moves to the▶ corner of the building.

3

◀Group 1 races past Group 2. They find new cover. Now they can defend Group 2.

Behind enemy lines

Soldiers in training can head back to their base to eat. Eating food gives the soldiers **energy**. Soldiers need energy to move about. Training hard uses lots of energy. But how do soldiers survive behind enemy lines?

All soldiers have survival rations in their packs. Survival rations are packets of food. The food does not weigh much. But it gives the soldiers enough energy to keep going.

Sometimes soldiers have to be able to eat quickly. Some food packs even heat up after pulling a tab!

Survival rations▶ give soldiers all the energy they need.

digestive system   parts of the body that break food down into useful parts

The food in survival rations is full of **nutrients**. Our bodies need nutrients for energy and growth. Food is broken down by your body to get the nutrients. This is done by your **digestive system**. The diagram below shows how it works.

One of the survival rations is chicken and rice. After being eaten, a liquid in the stomach breaks down the food. Nutrients are then taken into the blood through the small intestine.

The digestive system

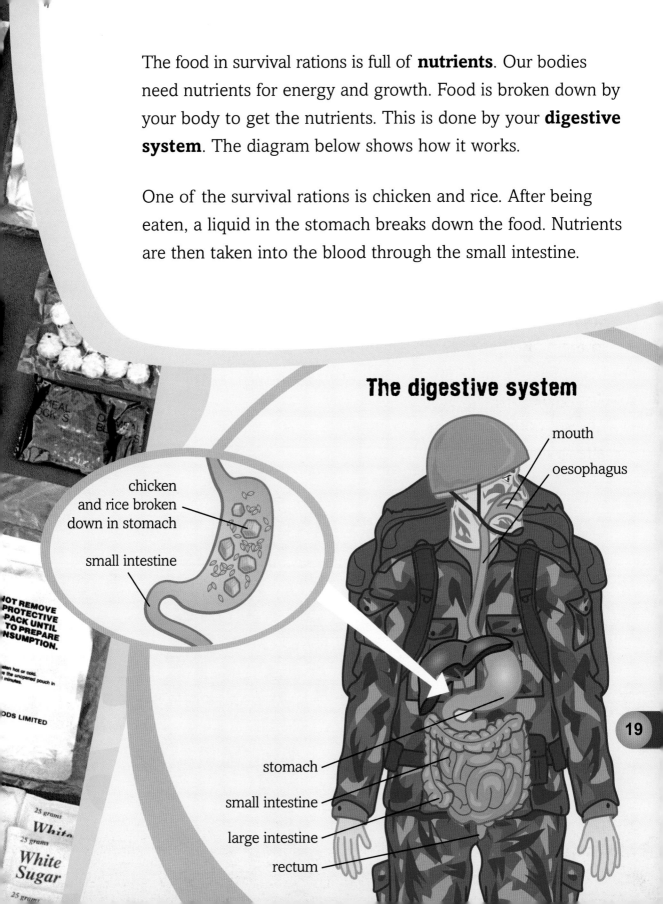

chicken and rice broken down in stomach

small intestine

mouth

oesophagus

stomach

small intestine

large intestine

rectum

Refuelling

There are **nutrients** in survival rations. Nutrients give a soldier **energy**. But how does the energy from the food get from the **digestive system** to the parts of the body that need it?

The nutrients are taken into the blood by the soldier's digestive system. Blood travels around our bodies in tubes called blood vessels. The blood is pumped around our bodies by an **organ** called the **heart**. An organ is a part of the body that does a special job. The heart and the blood vessels make up the **circulatory system**. The diagram below shows how it works.

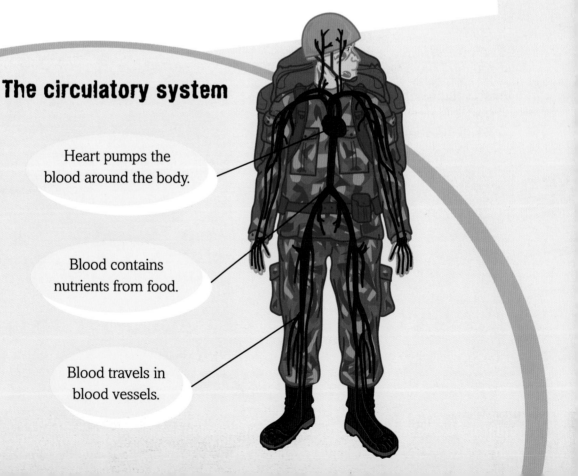

The circulatory system

Heart pumps the blood around the body.

Blood contains nutrients from food.

Blood travels in blood vessels.

◀ Survival rations are made of high-energy foods such as tuna fish and noodles.

circulatory system heart and blood vessels that move blood around the body

organ part of the body that does a special job

Breathing easy

These recruits are on a training run. To make things tougher, soldiers sometimes have to sing as they run along. This makes them even more out of breath!

Why do the soldiers get out of breath? Because they need more air! There is a gas in the air that our bodies need. This gas is called **oxygen**. Oxygen helps the body get **energy** from **nutrients**. The **muscles** need energy to work. The soldiers could not keep running if they did not have oxygen.

These soldiers are breathing ▶ quickly. Oxygen from the air will help get energy to the soldiers' muscles.

oxygen gas that helps the body get energy from nutrients

These recruits are ▼ breathing hard. Their bodies are using a lot of oxygen as they run.

24

lungs   parts of the body where oxygen gets into the blood

Getting fitter

Why do soldiers have to go on training runs? Because they need to be able to run or walk long distances without getting tired! They have to keep their **respiratory systems** fit by training.

The respiratory system allows us to breathe. Air goes into **organs** called **lungs** when we breathe. The lungs take the **oxygen** from the air that we breathe in. Then, the lungs supply the blood with oxygen.

Our lungs also help to remove carbon dioxide when we breathe out. Carbon dioxide is a gas that our bodies do not need.

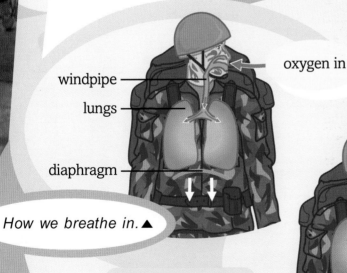

The respiratory system

oxygen in

windpipe

lungs

diaphragm

How we breathe in. ▲

carbon dioxide out

windpipe

lungs

diaphragm

Key:
- → oxygen
- → carbon dioxide

▲ *How we breathe out.*

25

What would you be?

So, are you tough enough for the armed forces?
What type of soldier would you like to be?

- An infantry soldier? You will need a strong **skeleton** and **muscles** for carrying your massive pack.

- A paratrooper? You will need strong muscles and **joints** for when you land on the ground.

- A special-forces expert? You will need a strong **heart** and **lungs** to keep moving behind enemy lines for days on end.

- An alpine soldier? You will need to be very fit for your body **systems** to work well in cold temperatures.

Infantry solders ▶ have to carry heavy packs.

▼ Paratroopers need strong leg muscles and bones for when they land.

Special forces soldiers ▲ must be able to survive behind enemy lines.

Alpine troops ▶ need to have good fitness levels.

What do you think? Which would you be? Whatever you choose, your body systems will have to be in great shape. Do you think you are tough enough?

Rescue mission

Here is one last mission! Your job is to rescue a prisoner. You're going to need all your body **systems** to do it.

STAGE 1

6 a.m.: You and five other soldiers must make a parachute drop into the snow. You will need a strong **skeleton** and **muscles** for when you hit the ground.

STAGE 2

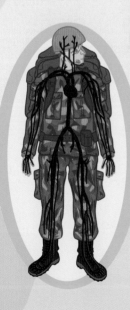

Get to the edge of the town by 4 p.m. Lie low at the bridge until midnight. This will be a good time to have something to eat. Your **digestive system** will need to take in some **energy**. Your **circulatory system** will then take this energy around your body to your muscles.

STAGE 3

Run across the bridge at midnight. Leave one soldier behind to guard your escape. Let's hope your **respiratory system** is up to the sprinting!

STAGE 4

Head for the Town Hall. Find the trap door leading into the cellar. One of you will have to hold the heavy trap door open. Pick the soldier with the strongest skeleton and muscles. The other soldiers must rescue a prisoner from the cellar.

STAGE 5

Carry the rescued prisoner back over the bridge.

STAGE 6

Run through the woods and find the clearing. At 5.30 p.m. a helicopter will land to take you back to base.

Glossary

circulatory system the heart and blood vessels that move blood around the body.

contract become smaller and tighter. A muscle contracts to move a part of your body.

digestive system parts of the body that break food down into useful parts. This system also gets rid of what is not needed.

energy ability to move something or to do work. Humans get their energy from the nutrients in food.

heart muscle that pumps blood around the body. The heart is the engine that powers the circulatory system.

joint place where two bones are linked together. Joints allow the body to bend and take in shocks.

lungs parts of the body where oxygen gets into the blood. The lungs are an important part of the respiratory system.

muscles parts of the body that allow a joint to move. Every moving joint in the body has at least two muscles.

nutrients parts of food that the body needs for growth and energy. Nutrients move around the body in the blood.

organ part of the body that does a special job. The eyes are organs that let us see.

oxygen gas that helps the body get energy from nutrients. The lungs take in oxygen from the air we breathe.

respiratory system parts of the body that allow us to breathe. The lungs are the core part of this system.

skeleton system of bones that gives the body its shape. The skeleton allows the body to carry heavy weights.

system parts of the body that work together to do something. The bones in a skeleton make up a system that gives support to the body.

Want to know more?

There's a lot to know about the human body! These are some great places to look:

Books

- *The Encyclopedia of the Human Body* (Dorling Kindersley, 2002)
- *The Human Body*, Ed. Martyn Page (Dorling Kindersley, 2005)

Movies and DVDs

- *Gallipoli* tells the story of two rival Australian sprinters who go to fight in the First World War.

Websites

- www.kidshealth.org/kid/body/digest _noSW.html looks at how the digestive system works.
- www.kidshealth.org/kid/body/heart _noSW.html can tell you more about how your heart works.
- Look inside the human body at www4.tpgi.com.au/users/amcgann/ body

Training for the Top tells you how top sportspeople get their bodies healthier and fitter – and how you can too!

Would You Survive? shows you how animals and plants manage to live where people cannot.

Index